THE JOY OF HOME

THE JOY OF HOME

Ashley Gilbreath

WRITTEN WITH ALICE WELSH DOYLE
AND BARRETT GILBREATH

PHOTOGRAPHY BY EMILY FOLLOWILL

FOREWORD BY JAMES T. FARMER III

Gibbs Smith

Contents

Foreword

I knew Ashley Freeman and Barrett Gilbreath at Auburn University. Ashley and I had some interior design courses together, graduated, and became design professionals. Ashley became Ashley Freeman Gilbreath and a rock star to me—an inspiration and the hardest working professional in the industry. She and Barrett have designed, decorated, and transformed homes from Montgomery to the mountains to the Gulf for their family, let alone many homes designed by Ashley and her excellent team for their clients.

Chic and classic, precise detail, and a sensational mix of antiques and contemporary style come to mind when I think of Ashley's attentive design direction. Beyond the pretty pleats and handsome lines, balances of the old and new, a delightful complement of textures and tones, there's an element to my friend's signature and skillfulness that extends beyond her expertise in the practice of interior design. Ashley is a true friend with a good heart, and that is evident in her work and relationships and intentions.

The ink was barely dry on our diplomas when Ashley and I had incredible opportunities early in our careers with trusting clients, publications taking a chance on a couple of young designers, and collaborations that made working together more like fun than work. One of the first projects we collaborated on was Barrett and Ashley's home in Montgomery. She had the interiors handled and I was shooting from the hip about some garden ideas. I remember we were standing in the yard of this home in the Old Cloverdale neighborhood and were finishing one another's sentences about railings, shades of creamy white paint, boxwoods, and gravel and how we loved nothing more than a courtyard like Mr. A. Hays Town would design back in Louisiana where Ashley grew up, and the landscape plan began to take shape with a sketchbook.

But one question Ashley asked me was so touching. It wasn't concerning plant material, shutters, or paint colors. Intentionally and heartfelt, she asked how I was doing. A designer's workday is rarely 9 to 5 and cookie cutter. We are involved in our clients' homes and thus their lives. So, that day it struck me that my dear friend was asking me about my life. The Gilbreaths and I had shared seasons of familial loss, and grief can bond people—especially when a connection stems from genuine love for our families. That love fuels passion for our practice and art.

Collaborations inside and outdoors became truly delightful projects with Ashley because I am always amazed by her work ethic, organization, and ability to move mountains effortlessly! I always knew that if I needed to talk to her for wisdom and advice, the need would be met by simply asking what she would do. Ashley's style is admirable and authentic, and that derives from her good nature.

Now we've each been practicing design, building and renovating houses for almost twenty years. Magazines have photographed the ways we decorate our homes for the holidays, and we work with fantastic architects and tradesmen all over the country. I can call Ashley for advice on nearly anything, and I know she'll impart said advice precisely and efficiently. From design service agreements, photo shoots, lighting companies, and even real estate, I have sought Ashley's advice. A professional colleague is helpful, but a friend is an outstanding treasure. And now, I am thrilled to call this college pal, design colleague, dear friend, and mountain neighbor a fellow author!

Here's to your new book, Ashley, and I look forward to all the great places it will take you. I'm thankful that as your friend, I have a front-row perspective.

—*James T. Farmer III*

Introduction

I grew up in Baton Rouge, Louisiana, and the refrains of my childhood resonated with the ideals of living graciously and making the most of what you have been given. My grandmother and mother had high standards; both felt anything undertaken should be done to the best of your ability. My mother is a proper and polished Southern lady who focused on teaching her children to give their all, to have kindness in their behavior, and to be always mindful of Southern hospitality. But since she had traveled the world for eighteen years as a flight attendant for Pan Am, she also encouraged us to have a sense of possibility and adventure. Being content to sit at home was not part of her recipe for living the best life possible.

My father was raised in rural Tennessee in a third-generation farmhouse, and his views were shaped by Depression-era values. When he spent money, it was very intentional. He is from a quiet family, but when he speaks, it's because he has something important to share. When I was a child, he would ask me if I could laugh at myself, if I had friends, if I could draw a picture; he viewed success in life through a different lens from my mother. They balanced each other well, and I have a deep appreciation for both their views.

When given the opportunity, my mother chose meaningful pieces for our home, touchstones in her memory. Reared to make a home as beautiful as possible by using available resources, my mother often asked me to restyle the bookcases and rearrange the furniture to bring out the best. As many Southerners do, she also had great respect for the treasures of the past imbued with family sentimentality and memory. My mother knows the provenance of every piece of furniture in our home, whether it came from my father's farmhouse or was handed down from a

member of her family, or where and why it was purchased. In fact, my daughter, Liza, sleeps in her great-great-grandfather's brass bed (also my childhood bed) from my father's farm.

My parents' values have certainly shaped my approach to decorating a home with a respect for tradition and an eye on practicality and warmheartedness. Now, with a family of my own, I strive to provide my children with the same gracious environment and instill in them an appreciation for our time as a family. Personal style is often rooted in childhood memories, and those memories and feelings will shape a family's experience. Evocative remembrances—such as the sound of a crackling fireplace, enticing aromas from the kitchen, grandmother's needlepoint pillows, mother's dressing table, and certain colors—influence how we want to live in our homes. I aim to create casual spaces with an elegant ease, where families gather to celebrate the same joy in everyday living that I experienced growing up.

For every project, I focus on creating a home tailored to each family's needs and to stand the test of time. I tap into my clients' histories and memories to understand what resonates with them. Weaving together their past and present allows me to create spaces not only to evoke past happy family memories but also to lay a foundation for the future. All my thought and planning are infused with functionality, comfort, and beauty in mind. It is such an honor to be invited into people's lives to help shape a little piece of what we take with us—our memories. I view my role as an opportunity to guide the daily experiences of each family. Design is about more than just colors and objects, but rather about emotion; home can be a joyful stage set for the memories of life.

Each home burgeons with a mixture of influences: pieces with a history and pieces with history to be made; thoughtful floor planning, texture, color, and details; and custom pieces in harmony with our clients' visions. Having a family of my own helps me to keep it real. My design firm focuses on the selection of materials to survive the rough-and-tumble of family living without sacrificing beauty and charm. Many of our clients come to us with an initial hesitation about "having nice things" with young children at home. I love these conversations because it provides me an opportunity to showcase a thoughtful and practical approach to our work, and it makes the finished product so much more enjoyable when our clients realize we made this dream a reality.

Throughout this book, you will see a variety of house styles and locations, from elegant city homes to lakeside and beach retreats. Each project shows how I approach the decorating process with the clients' goals as the jumping-off point. I take their list of wants, dial into their happy memories and passions, and translate them into a studied mix of furnishings, color, fabrics, and décor.

You'll discover how I create a balance between formal and informal, between comfort and elegance in two very different houses; how I incorporated a client's favorite color throughout one home and used an understated neutral palette in another. A tour of my personal family beach home shows injections of color and pattern as I explain my thought processes.

While the clients' tastes dictate most decisions, you'll also see some of my signature design strategies in play: a liberal use of drapery to highlight and disguise; eclectic mixes of art pieces; carefully selected light fixtures; timeworn antiques alongside reproductions and vintage finds; and favorite custom treatments, such as banquettes at dining tables and dressmaker details on chairs.

Whether it's in town, at the beach, or in the mountains, everything I do as a designer comes from a passion for gracious everyday living. I feel truly privileged to create joyful and memorable spaces for each phase of a family's journey in this life and beyond and to make their dreams of home come true. I hope this book inspires and helps you discover your own personal design style so the rooms you put together resonate with meaning and create a joyful home.

The Color Connection

Color is very personal and can be a mood changer in a room, providing a beautiful background for any atmosphere. It can add calm sophistication on one hand and upbeat cheer on the other. I think the common fear of color stems from misunderstanding, the belief that color will take over a room.

Growing up in the South, my recollection of color in design is most vivid from visits to my grandparents' houses. Later, I remember my mom incorporating certain pieces in our home as she held onto the memories of her own childhood. Florals, stripes, and even paisleys found their way into action, each a proud contribution to the eclectic story our home told. While those memories of color are a bit more distant these days, I remember it always being tasteful and never overdone.

I try to teach moderation with my children, and color in design is no different; a little can go a long way! With any color, the supporting cast is very important. The smallest details, such as the color of a book jacket placed on a cocktail table or the flange on a pillow, ultimately interpret the color story. Everything is in focus, and the goals are balance and intention. Embracing color doesn't have to mean living in a kaleidoscope, but done well, it can be incredibly uplifting.

Working with architects, like C. Brandon Ingram, who designed this house, is always a privilege. What started as a whole-home renovation quickly turned into a

An elegant entry stairway with detailed millwork didn't require much decoration. A French armchair and a series of artworks allow the architectural details to take center stage.

The study is one of the first focal points inside the front door. A vintage chinoiserie screen, an octagon cocktail table, and a Spanish writing desk bring some welcome patina into the room, juxtaposed with a contemporary painting by artist William McLure.

From the hand-painted wall covering and the custom cornices to simple, elegant chairs and the crystal chandelier, it is all in the details for this formal dining room.

ABOVE: A skirted vanity with simple tailored details adds a welcome softness to the colorful and playful chinoiserie wall covering. OPPOSITE: The color-saturated scullery began the whole color conversation in the home, and this shade is carried throughout.

The custom banquette, which can handle a crowd, and a mix of an antique drop leaf dining table, a set of four vintage chairs (once red but painted for this setting), and a bamboo plant stand tastefully complete the sunny breakfast space.

I try to teach moderation with my children, and color in design is no different; a little can go a long way!

new build using only the existing foundation footprint of the previous structure. The final product is both elegant and classic. Impactful color and chinoiserie meld with more traditional elements of the architecture to strike the perfect connection to a vivacious personality.

The vibrant coral hue throughout the home is used to create cohesion while also injecting a bit of levity and nonchalance into the classical architecture. Proper color usage allows for natural progression through interior spaces and provides segues to outdoor living areas. The scullery—the primary application of the featured color—can be seen from many angles, so finding the perfect shade was crucial in creating proper tonality at various times of day and in the presence of natural light. Having such an impactful color as a unifying thread is an intuitive way to achieve continuity of space without it feeling overwrought or matchy. Neutral grass cloth on the walls provides just the right amount of calm and balance in the space while allowing the inspiration color to remain the focal point. We were able to weave the color into the window treatments of the rear entry, lamps in the dining room, art in the study, and in light punches in the powder bath wall covering.

Every space on the primary level received some amount of direction from the color-heart of the home. Balance is clearly key when using a strong focal color, and

OPPOSITE: An antique, color-rich rug pulls the tone from the scullery into the more neutral kitchen. OVERLEAF: Leather-upholstered counter stools and a pair of brass-trimmed pendants add elegance to a very functional kitchen.

Luxurious bed drapings complete with a tailored, pleated valance offer a warm embrace. We recovered our client's settee in a pale, loose stripe that easily slipped into the room.

ABOVE: An intentionally oversized mirror adds a layer of depth to this vignette.
OPPOSITE: Custom, sculptural demilune tables, along with vintage chinoiserie lamps
paired with pleated silk shades, bring an artful note to the main bedroom.

Having even small doses of impactful color is an intuitive way to achieve continuity of space without it feeling overwrought or matchy.

the kitchen and breakfast area's position adjacent the scullery required creamy neutrals to achieve it. The equilibrium then allows for visual transition to the greens and blues of the garden and pool area. In the dining room, we went a bit more formal by mixing in some period antiques, a crystal chandelier, and a French mirror, all with a hand-painted, neutral, chinoiserie wall covering serving as a backdrop. White fretwork dining chairs were chosen to keep the room from being too serious.

Early in my career, while commenting how easily I could pick out the fabulous works of certain designers in various publications, a much more seasoned colleague quickly remarked how those projects ultimately said more about the designers than their clients. I recommitted then to design spaces for our clients using their thoughts and memories, ensuring continuity and balance in their transition to their new living spaces. Rather than imposing my style on anyone, I use my experience to ensure the proper application and utility of our clients' styles. In the end, the successful use of a client-selected, vibrant color and proper balance resulted in a thoughtfully designed home filled with joy and intrigue.

OPPOSITE: A classic white bathroom never goes out of fashion. Brass faucets, hardware, sconces, and a large, pale blue lantern add definition. An antique chair, a coral-hued runner, and a classic blue-and-white chinoiserie side table keep the room from reading too stark. OVERLEAF LEFT: Custom bunk beds in a sophisticated pink provide plenty of room for sleepovers. OVERLEAF RIGHT: A daughter's bedroom is not too childish to grow with her. Subtle prints and tailored details give it longevity.

OPPOSITE: No matter what door you enter through, the coral color story is seen from the moment you walk in. ABOVE: Colorful, patterned wall covering paired with coordinating cabinets and unique light fixtures make laundry a little less daunting.

Beautiful and classic architecture sets the tone for this house—inside and out.

Restrained Elegance

I am no stranger to home renovation; my husband and I have lived in an embarrassingly high number of houses over the last two decades. But I often say that renovating a house is the key talent God gave me. While many of our client jobs are ground-up new construction, our team loves working with talented architects and contractors on renovation projects to keep us on our toes. With renovations, there are always a few unforeseen issues to be addressed, and decisions are made on-site and on the fly.

Wish lists, however, don't have to be for the sake of preexisting conditions. The wish list for this project was short and sweet: sophisticated and luxurious entertaining spaces. This is not to suggest that these rooms can't be enjoyed and lived in, but rather to point out the focus of the detail shifts slightly from function to form. After all, how elegant could we be without a pair of stunning yet slightly uncomfortable shoes?

To entertain guests on the lower level of this renovation, architect David Baker of Tippett Sease Baker created a certain level of intrigue with a new staircase complete with paneled walls and a custom railing leading to a moody but warm

A sculptural armchair makes an inviting spot for a pause, and a new iron stair rail added during the renovation gives the stairway a simplistic statement.

A pair of custom upholstered cabinets with nailhead trim dress up the fireplace wall in the living room.

A mix of finishes, including a wooden table with a marble base, a textured wall covering, a vintage gilded mirror, and a custom concrete console table keep the eye engaged in the dining room.

OPPOSITE: A leather chandelier brings a glamorous and unexpected note to the dining room. The gray-hued wall covering is a rich backdrop for subtle decorative accents such as a brass candelabra and framed art. OVERLEAF: Wood accents and hair-on-hide counter stools bring a welcome softness to the kitchen.

A custom banquette along with antique barley twist chairs slipcovered
in a performance fabric welcome a crowd in this breakfast room.

Custom pieces designed specifically for a home are worth the investment. While fitting in seamlessly, they also impart a luxurious distinction that gives reason to pause and admire the craftsmanship.

area below grade. A wine room and a fireside sitting area help make this space a magnetic enclave for both pre- and post-dinner conversation.

On the main level, the style is grown-up. A rich, dark gray, textured wall covering sets a sumptuous tone, and the mood of the entire space can be easily exaggerated by candlelight. Dramatic lighting and clean-lined seating options are inviting. The quiet color palette subtly weaves in a lovely shade of green throughout.

A wood cocktail table and a stone fireplace surround complement an oversized piece of contemporary art to create a quiet and engaging atmosphere. A pair of tall, upholstered cabinets flank the fireplace and offer a luxurious distinction, giving reason to pause and admire the craftsmanship. Scale and proportion are key factors in creating the appropriate and desired level of decorum in the living room.

An oversized custom hood together with a marble-slab backsplash in the kitchen elevate the attitude of the space. Pale gray cabinetry maintains the level of sophistication carried throughout the home. And while a custom banquette was

A design objective of creating coziness is achieved with deep green paint on the walls, ceiling, and trim and high-backed wing chairs perfect for reading. An oversized, patinaed floor mirror reflects light around the room, making it feel larger, and a silk-tasseled light fixture adds interest.

A blend of textures used throughout the main bedroom all work timelessly together to create a curated look. OVERLEAF LEFT: An antique console and a black Empire-style armchair join for a chic moment in the main bedroom. OVERLEAF RIGHT: A nickel-plated soaking tub is the star of this bathroom.

OPPOSITE: A custom foxed mirror with iron details makes an impactful statement in the den and adds depth to the setting. ABOVE: In a streamlined design, art is an especially important layering element. These contemporary pieces were commissioned specifically for this den.

Rooms we create specifically for children and grandchildren allow those who use them to feel a sense of place and true destination.

added in the breakfast area for just the right touch of elegance, the treated performance fabric will still allow for family gatherings and the occasional stray droplet from a coffee mug or red wine glass.

The small library—perfect for more intimate gatherings—features a collection of stools to be used as seating or ottomans. The tasseled chandelier fosters immediate conversation, and the green-painted wall paneling and ceiling engender an open invitation to sit a spell.

Not totally abandoning the younger members of the family, the upper floor serves as an oasis for when children need to retreat somewhere slightly more familiar. These rooms we created specifically for children and grandchildren allow those who use it to feel a sense of place and true destination.

Elegant. Luxurious. Intriguing. Inspiring. While this full-scale renovation is decidedly more sophisticated than some, I know the joy experienced and the memories created in this home are measurable and memorable.

Bird-motif wall covering brings a little whimsy to the laundry room. A vintage-style refrigerator is handy for grabbing a beverage when heading outside.

This bunkroom with its
cheerful blue palette and
coral accent lamps makes for
a dreamy setting. The writing
table with low-profile
upholstered stools is ideal for
art projects and homework.

A vintage, overscaled, framed chalkboard along with a table and chairs create a play area, while the stripe-painted floor adds an intentional detail carried throughout the room.

Gracious Lakeside Simplicity

Location is always a consideration when starting a project, but it's especially critical when the surroundings are the ultimate reason for the home's existence. Some people call them second homes and some vacation homes. To me, the homes where we go to get away could be described as "journey homes." Life is a journey, not a destination.

My father-in-law always says it's important to enjoy the journey, and if we are to enjoy the journey of life, we must set aside the time it takes to reflect and appreciate. My childhood family never owned a journey home, but I remember trips to the Grand Hotel on Mobile Bay in Point Clear, Alabama, and the rustic feeling of the lobby. There was a grand, three-sided fireplace where we used to wait eagerly for another log to be thrown on the crackling fire. No matter the reason for the visit, I always felt like our family left there happier with each other and generally happier to return home to everyday life.

To me, lake living is peaceful and still, enlivened by the humming chorus of crickets and grasshoppers. Owned by the family for decades, this lake property was transformed by architect Chris Tippett of Tippett Sease Baker into a welcoming retreat and a cradle of priceless memories. The house slips seamlessly

The décor takes cues from nature as well as the organic materials used in the architecture. Stone and white oak impart rustic warmth, which are picked up in the rich brown leather armchairs and pale wheat-hued upholstery.

For a more casual feel in the dining area, I paired two types of comfortable chairs: linen-slipcovered armchairs and cane-backed dining chairs in a subtle plaid. The overall look is gracious and simple.

RIGHT: The white oak, recessed panel wall serves as one of the many architectural focal points in the room. It also hides the TV. OVERLEAF: Green mohair chairs and large copper jugs wired as lamps commune with the outdoors.

While we always love incorporating antiques, mixing in new upholstery and some of the owners' existing sentimental pieces creates balance.

and respectfully into the landscape and incorporates the surroundings into the living space.

The home is understated and comfortable, yet sophisticated. We used a varied mix of new and vintage furnishings to create a sense of place without being cliché on the lake theme. Rustic refinement was our focus, using quiet, reflective colors to enhance the spectacular views of the window-filled rooms. The interior design needed only to enhance, not detract, starting its reveal slowly after the initial, serene feeling of taking in the views.

Harmonious neutrals—browns, grays, and olives—along with textures of linen, leather, and wood are all at home here. Additional inspiration was drawn from the use of stone and white oak in several noteworthy architectural details. Both the architecture and design refrain from complexity, allowing Nature's beauty to carry the day.

While we wanted this design to feel relaxing and casual, we didn't shy away from using a few understated antiques and vintage pieces to create a sense of history, personality, and sentiment. A beautiful, clean-lined, antique armoire in the master bedroom, perfectly worn leather chairs in the family room, and an

The kitchen stands out while still being a part of the whole. The metal hood and soapstone backsplash give it distinction; the white oak island nods to the adjoining spaces; and the brass light feature adds a polished note.

ABOVE: A cozy breakfast nook combines a custom banquette with quirky vintage chairs covered in cowhide. People hesitate to use whole hides, but keep in mind that cows lie down in mud—this durable seat covering will outlast anything else in the house! OPPOSITE: The working pantry tucks essentials out of the way in a handsome cabinet with soapstone counters and cabinetry with metal mesh fronts. OVERLEAF: The main bedroom is a play on tone and layer. The dark wall color cocoons, while the white bedding and furniture soothe.

LEFT: A bleached armoire creates a focal point in the room along with an added sense of warmth. It also doubles as hidden storage for the TV. ABOVE: A 19th-century Spanish writing desk makes an intimate vignette for quiet reflection or private journaling.

ABOVE: The white oak main bathroom vanity holds hands with a patinaed and scalloped vintage piece. The completely windowed vanity wall required a little ingenuity. Sheer Roman shades keep the view ever present. OPPOSITE: A soaking tub takes full advantage of the views.

OPPOSITE: A guest room reveals layers of texture—a woven bedside table, a slip-covered, rush-seated side chair, and a sisal rug. The four-poster bed adds definition, while horizontally striped drapery keeps the mood light. ABOVE: Brass accents in the monochromatic powder bath add a bit of elegance in an otherwise moody enclave.

Upstairs, a playroom–bunk space adjoins guest suites so adults can keep an eye on the young visitors. Comfortable, neutral upholstery grounded by a jaunty, durable, striped rug and a fabric-wrapped pendant welcomes cozy respite after a lively day on the lake.

*There's a sense of being still at the
lake, enlivened by the humming chorus
of crickets and grasshoppers.*

outstanding old bench in the side entry all serve as key characters in the story we created. While we always love incorporating antiques, mixing in new upholstery and some of the owners' existing sentimental pieces creates balance.

I was deliberate when choosing the art so as not to compete with God's natural palette. Not wanting any pieces to overpower a space, I eschewed boldly colored works in favor of botanical prints and nature-inspired designs in partnership with the exterior. Restrained choices blend in while still adding interest and texture—Italian olive oil vessels, woven baskets and trays, and antler sheds are sparingly used decorative touches.

Practicality informed our choices as well. Treated fabrics allow for wet swimsuits, and family-friendly sisal and striped wool rugs can withstand lake life. Yet, for the inevitable entertaining of family and friends, an unobtrusive elegance shines through in graciously lined furnishings, iron chandeliers, and lamps with noteworthy gravitas. The open floor plan includes a round dining table and a generous mix of places to perch, inviting convivial gatherings. Everything is in harmony with nature and living in rustic refinement, ready to capture a host of new memories while enjoying the journey.

OPPOSITE: The side entry welcomes with a very special find: a divided antique bench that can hold guests' bags or offer a place to sit down and put on shoes. OVERLEAF: It's all about outdoor living at the lake, with dining and lounging spaces to soak in the view.

Personal
& Polished

I remember when my husband and I purchased our first "forever house." Yes, I totally understand most normal people have one forever house—that's the point. But I now realize I haven't yet lived in mine, and maybe it will be a while before I do. However, when we bought the first one, everything had to be perfect. It wasn't, but I felt like it should be. Though we didn't have children yet, I imagined them being there. I thought through nurseries and toddler rooms, preteen and high school rooms. I considered the need for a small outbuilding suitable for a little girl's playhouse and even thought about wedding receptions in our backyard! It's amazing how far our minds can go when we start thinking about the distant future. Designing forever houses for our clients is a thrill that lets me relive those feelings I had so many years ago.

When a young couple purchases their forever house, the initial conversations usually revolve around needed changes—a dated kitchen and bathrooms, an awkward floor plan, and finishes stuck in time. Ideally, there are redeeming architectural features and details—good bones—to be used as a starting point. In this instance, we were fortunate to have a beautiful shell; we just needed to make it personal. We were able to avoid all the renovation conversations and focus on

Stacking different types of artworks instead of using just one large piece or a tall mirror can draw the eye up and give a feeling of height. These are all landscapes, so they speak to each other in a meaningful way while having a distinct accent.

Undoubtedly, the specific usage of individual spaces will evolve over time, but I hope their purpose—creating lasting memories—remains the same.

purchasing items to express how the couple wanted to live in the home. The selections we made should fill a specific need now and be able to mature with the family over time. Our focus was scale, proportion, durability, and function to create cozy and inviting spaces to last a lifetime. I'm sure the specific usage of individual spaces will evolve over time, but I hope their purpose—creating lasting memories—remains the same.

With small children at home, performance fabrics are a must, especially for spaghetti nights and chocolate-covered fingers. Durable and treatable, these fabrics make it possible to avoid sacrificing beauty and nice things for fear of them being ruined. You can absolutely have your cake and eat it too! One such "nice thing" was an antique plate rack for displaying fine china, which I picked up on a buying trip to Italy. For this application, we hung the rack in the kitchen and displayed the children's artwork instead of dinner plates. This rotating, color-filled art gallery is not only an area of pride for the little ones but also emphasizes their special contribution to the feel and design of a room. As the children get older, the artwork may become more and more sophisticated, or perhaps evolve

PREVIOUS OVERLEAF AND OPPOSITE: In the dining room, we turned vintage, patinaed, green plant stands into buffet lamps, which serve as interesting foils to the grand crystal chandelier. The bleached antique buffet creates a perfect juxtaposition to the polished dining room table.

ABOVE AND OPPOSITE: The study already had beautiful pecky cypress walls and built-ins, so we wanted to add some darker pieces for more definition. An old Spanish-style trestle table serves as the desk, joined by a skirted, olive-green leather desk chair and a large custom foxed mirror. OVERLEAF: Since the family gathers to watch TV in this room but also entertains here, it needed to be comfortable with a brushstroke of elegance. We included a slipcovered sofa, armchairs with pretty, sinewy lines, and a durable leather ottoman to be moved around as needed.

OPPOSITE: Over the antique chests flanking the fireplace, we suspended a fabric wall hanging to aid in reducing the scale of the mantel and the ceiling height.

The large kitchen had a great floor plan and impressive architectural finishes. To impart some softness, we introduced striped slipcovers on the chairbacks and added upholstered counter stools in the same treated fabric.

OPPOSITE: Lining the backs of glass-front cabinets with fabric imparts a welcome softness in a sea of hard surfaces.

Incorporating children's artwork into our designs is ideal for adding personal and joyful color elements. The children enjoy being celebrated in this way, and the antique plate rack makes swapping out the work a breeze!

If you purchase a home with blessed good bones, you are already ahead of the curve. You are freer to focus on making choices that simply speak to your lifestyle and decorating passions.

into a collage of family photos, eventually giving way to collections of china. Or maybe it will remain a place of fond reflection on the innocence of childhood.

The antique breakfast room table already tells a story with its perfect imperfections and will only be enhanced by the unavoidable new character marks added over the next several years. The adjacent dining room is slightly more elegant and polished, suitable for baby doll tea parties and family holiday gatherings alike. These two spaces so close to one another provide suitable overflow for the inevitable, and occasionally coveted, kids table.

When I think about the traditional definition of the forever house, and perhaps my inability to stay in one, I am reminded how temporary a house can be in contrast to our recollections of things we experienced and how we felt there. I may, in fact, never have the traditional forever house, but I look forward to my eternal house full of family and wonderful memories.

A functional hallway has been elevated to gallery status with the strategic placement of artwork suspended on decorative brass art brackets.

In the main bedroom, we included whispers of blue and green in the upholstery and bedding, the same hues that are seen throughout the house, creating a common thread.

110

Juxtaposition & Balance

My father grew up in a third-generation farmhouse in Brownsville, Tennessee. He still owns the small farm and house today. He often talks about going down to the "bottom" and fishing with cane poles and chasing deer and rabbits through the woods with BB guns. He liked recounting these stories to remind us as children there was an alternative to the city life we lived in Baton Rouge. It seems we always found ways to incorporate country living in every season. We walked to the small neighborhood pond to feed ducks; we had small vegetable plots in our backyard; we would go down to the spillways in the bayou and fish for red drum; we took pirogues back in the swamp to check crawfish traps; we even raised a baby squirrel we found after a storm. All these activities are fond memories for me, in part because they were such a diversion from our daily routine, but mostly because it was time I got to spend with my dad. My parents always thought life in the city pulled against the time we got to spend as a family. As often as possible, we had meals as a family, and our home was always a place of refuge.

I hope my design work always goes deeper than the pieces purchased for a home or the colors put on the walls. My work is intended to balance form and function with memory and emotion as I help make a house a home.

Repeating lanterns balance the architecture and serve as an introduction to the living and dining room. To the left of the entrance, a patinaed, antique demilune table in a connecting space makes a pretty statement without being too precious or hands-off.

A mingling of textural elements surrounding an old wooden chest—a weathered stone sculpture, woven baskets, and a framed African mudcloth—bring quiet but expressive organic notes to the living room.

Juxtaposition and balance in design result in a home being at once comfortable and refined, family-friendly and elegant, polished and simple.

Juxtaposition and balance in design result in a home being at once comfortable and refined, family-friendly and elegant, polished and simple. We were fortunate to work with architect C. Brandon Ingram from the ground up on this project. Equilibrium in each space was achieved through the careful selection of fabrics, furnishings, lighting, and rugs. Overall, the home presents a welcome off-handedness—a collected and gathered look. Views of the beautiful, wooded lake setting beyond provide a sense of how the interiors should feel. Embracing the outdoors was paramount in creating harmony in this idyllic setting.

Generously proportioned spaces provide ample room for family gatherings, and we created visual vignettes without breaking up a room. An upholstered screen divides the living room and the dining space without abandoning connectedness. An English rolled-arm sofa finds company with a large wood-and-iron coffee table in harmony with the light fixture above. An antique trumeau mirror elevates a moment for more formal entertaining, while a less imposing starburst mirror hangs on a panel of the screen to dress up a more intimate seating arrangement. Treated fabric on the dining room host chairs matches the durability and staying power of the antique leather side chairs and provides protection from spills and daily use, and

The upholstered screen that separates the living room from the dining area is detailed with nailhead ornamentation creating a faux panel effect. OVERLEAF: Large, preserved botanicals framed between two pieces of glass are suspended from drapery rods to add interest at the window wall.

OPPOSITE: The dining space has a dressed up–dressed down presentation, with antique furnishings in patinaed finishes paired with a large, painted, French trumeau mirror and refined, high-back host chairs.

RIGHT: The kitchen's polished allure is tempered by classic ladder-back, rush-seat counter stools. OVERLEAF: An antique trestle table makes a good choice for a family breakfast space. We mixed seating options and fabrics to impart a more casual attitude, set off by a large rope-and-iron chandelier to make a powerful statement but in humble materials.

The keeping room pairs some of my favorite fabric selections, stripes and checks, along with a family-friendly performance velvet on the ottoman.

I hope my work always goes deeper than the pieces purchased for a home or the colors put on the walls. My work is intended to balance form and function with memory and emotion as I help make a house a home.

a large, custom banquette covered in treated raffia provides durable seating for a crowd in the less formal breakfast area.

We used color to evoke a casual sophisticated ease—a timeless and subtle palette with neutrals, pale blues, browns, greens, and grays sitting in graceful companionship with the nature outside. An exception to the otherwise calmly muted spaces is the office area with bold, smoky-green lacquered walls and cabinetry. Brass hardware and a leather chandelier complete this space with elegant refinement. All the fabrics throughout the home speak to stylish comfort. They are selectively informal—linen, cotton poplin, and other selections with textural appeal—and intentionally treated to serve as the literal foundation for family memories in every space.

This home is specifically designed for wholesome family togetherness. Being tucked away on a private lake setting reminded me of those stories I often heard from my dad. The ability to have a little slice of solitude just outside the city limits allows this family to more easily connect and recharge. We all need these moments to create balance in our lives and I am honored to be able to help in this pursuit.

The antique doors used in the butler's pantry are a rare find discovered on a buying trip in Italy. They are complemented by the high-gloss painted cabinets, brass hardware, and soapstone countertops.

OPPOSITE: A high-gloss smoky green wraps the walls, ceiling, and cabinetry for a glamour-infused effect in the library. ABOVE: A group of framed, vintage botanical prints speak to the beauty outside. OVERLEAF: The main bedroom includes a custom four-poster wooden bed, designed by Reid Classics, that leans a touch more masculine, while the details are a bit more feminine. PAGES 134–135: Simple materials combined with thoughtful detail in the painted millwork, tile design, and countertops add interest in this main bathroom.

Small details like the bed canopy, custom lamp shades, and vintage family crests hung above the bed create a thoughtful guest retreat.

Rocking chairs and a cozy rope swing on a bluestone-tiled porch off the breakfast room beckon to sit and stay awhile. The haint-blue porch ceiling keeps a Southern tradition.

Genteel Hospitality

My mother is the picture of Southern hospitality. She grew up in Ozark, Alabama, and has always spoken of how her mother treated everyone with grace and welcoming charm. I remember the feeling of warmth and the distinct nostalgic aroma every time we visited my grandparents when I was little. Later, after my grandparents passed away, my mother recalled those memories as she worked to provide the same feelings of hospitality to guests in our home. I remember bringing college friends home with me on long weekends and being greeted by a spread of hors d'oeuvres, sweets, and fresh fruit. There were fresh-cut flowers in every room, and overnight guests were treated with crystal bud vases at their bedside with single stems of gardenias or camellias, depending on the season. Mornings were enhanced by the fragrance of sizzling bacon in cast-iron skillets and the sweet and tangy taste of sugar-dusted grapefruit served with grandmother's sterling grapefruit spoons. Even now, when I go back home with my own family, all these things welcome me back as if I never left. There is something special about a Southern matriarch. I hope I can live up to the examples gone before me.

A common theme for many people when designing a home is the reflection on positive childhood memories of either a home in which they grew up or an often-visited home of a relative. These positive emotional responses are my focus during the initial brainstorming and design sessions. In this case, we were tasked with recreating—in emotional detail—a replica of memories from childhood.

A little alcove under the beautiful stairway provided an opportunity for a special moment; the aged finish on the chest perfectly reflects other hues in the rooms beyond. A porcelain lamp, ceramic vase, and contemporary art piece complete the vignette.

ABOVE: The foyer introduces the balance between formal and informal seen throughout the home. A sophisticated, pale blue damask wall covering pairs with a rush-seat bench, while an antique Oushak rug joins in. OPPOSITE: We placed a vintage suzani in the foyer to set the color tone for the rest of the house. Old textiles impart a sense of history, as well as provide a diverse mix of art in the home.

PREVIOUS OVERLEAF: The dining room has a fresh approach to everyday casual elegance, from the dressmaker details on the chairs, tailored and feminine cornices, and gilded, carved mirror and console to the more casual, natural sisal rug and open-air chandelier.
ABOVE: With the console table and mirror, an aged container takes down the formality.
OPPOSITE: An engaging mix springs from all the detail.

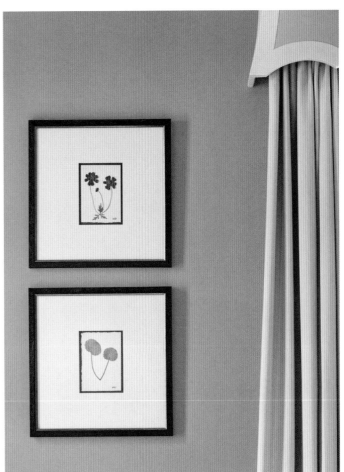

ABOVE: The artful layering of objects on a coffee table elevates the décor of this family room. OPPOSITE: The dark blue walls along with the Persian rug impart a sense of warmth that is carried throughout the space. A bold painting by Kayce Hughes brings lively color and a contemporary vibe to the antiques-filled room. OVERLEAF LEFT: The warm details in the antique secretary and its moiré lining add another level of sentiment to this family room. OVERLEAF RIGHT: A reading nook sits adjacent to the fireplace, creating a destination for the book lover.

OPPOSITE AND ABOVE: The keeping room adjoins the kitchen, serving as the heart of the home. Four upholstered chairs arranged around a tufted ottoman create an intimate place for family moments. The built-ins and millwork details add a soft texture to the walls, while magnolia from the yard is an intentional way of bringing the outside in.

A light blue grass cloth continued from the keeping room graces the walls. A custom vent hood and the Roman shades combine to draw the eye upward. The stacks of weathered breadboards have an organic quality and complete the symmetry of the entire wall.

OPPOSITE: Glass-front cabinetry adds a timeless detail in the kitchen while offering a display of our client's china collection. OVERLEAF: The breakfast room, open to the kitchen, is set apart by floral drapery and contrasting window trim. An antique scalloped bench intentionally fills the window wall and provides a comfortable backdrop for family dinners.

Southern hospitality toes the line between proper and relaxed. We "pull the string" to sit tall in our chairs for dinner, and we sink back into comfortable chairs with a glass of sweet tea for a conversation.

Coral pinks, burnt reds, blues, and botanical prints are used here, but in a slightly more updated fashion. The feeling is intentionally formal in certain places and less so in others, but still collectively cohesive. Balancing the elegant with the casual in a home requires a studied approach; the rooms need to be similar enough to recognize familial kinship but have distinct personalities and pleasant surprises.

A formal foyer serves as a well-mannered first impression but quickly gives way to an elegant blend of textures. The house is unmistakably traditional, in a Southern way, but not at all stuffy. Woven rush seats, wood finishes, wicker, natural rugs, and lively traditional prints offer warmth and a sense of well-being. A fireplace in the keeping room off the kitchen serves up nostalgia as it plays host to morning coffees and cozy chats. This connecting pass-through space becomes a destination, allowing a pause before traveling on your way.

The generous breakfast room returns as more refined. Linen portieres impart softness to the walls and can be drawn closed for more privacy and separation. Additional woven rush-seat chairs provide consistency but are elevated with blue slipcovers piped in coral. They are complemented by wicker head chairs, hearkening back to childhood memories. For uniqueness, I included a beautifully carved,

Slipcovers in a treated fabric provide a fresh update to the otherwise traditional rush-seat dining chair while also working to continue the color story used throughout the home.

The painted French chest of drawers adds storage to the breakfast room,
while the gilded Louis Phillipe mirror reflects daylight in the space.

A floral theme as seen in the headboard, vintage textile on the bed, and the framed preserved botanicals add a feminine touch in the main bedroom. The color palette here is an extension of the rest of the home.

Balancing the elegant with the casual requires a studied approach. Rooms need to be just similar enough to recognize familial kinship, but have distinct personalities and pleasant surprises.

scalloped-back bench with a family crest dating back to the seventeenth century. It tells its own family story and invites conversation while giving this new home a much-desired patina and collected appeal.

Deep blues and floral reds find their way into the palette in the wall covering, window treatments, and Persian rugs, but nothing feels overpowering or intimidating. A simple, natural rug, a skirted sofa, and streamlined sconces keep the spaces firmly balanced between formal and relaxed. Two exquisite antique corner cabinets, hidden from view until guests fully enter the room, provide another moment of intrigue without totally stealing the show. Window treatments with dressmaker details; an antique, marble-topped, gilded console; and a carved mirror share an air of elegance, while an airy chandelier and chairs with box-pleated slipcovers reinforce the traditional.

Southern hospitality toes the line between proper and relaxed. We "pull the string" to sit tall in our chairs with proper posture for dinner, and we sink back into more comfortable chairs with a glass of sweet tea as we talk about the weather and our sports team's performance. My grandmother and mother have elegantly modeled this blurred dichotomy for me with grace and dignity. I pray my daughters will one day feel the same way about their mother.

The dressing table is topped with an overscaled gilded mirror reflecting beautifully in the room. It is tempered by an iron chandelier and crisp white panels trimmed with a decorative tape.

An antique armoire, doubling as hidden storage for the TV, adds warmth to
the main bedroom. The chaise brings a layer of comfort.

On the Edge of Modern

In more than fifteen years on my own as a designer, I have been fortunate to have had projects all over the country. Imagine my excitement when I was presented the opportunity to work on a fabulous new build with an amazing architect and a fantastic builder—in a neighborhood in Baton Rouge where so many of my childhood memories were made. This neighborhood is in the heart of the city, a short drive east of the LSU campus. Arriving for site visits in this beautiful setting, canvased by the architectural influence of A. Hays Town and canopied by century-old live oaks, always gave me chills. My mom would often drive by the project and provide unsolicited updates on its progress. She even made sure my name was added to the job board posted near the street. While I am honored to be selected for any job in any location, this project in my hometown is an indelible memory.

Working with architect David Baker of Tippett Sease Baker always pushes me to be a little more edgy and even more mindful of the subtle details present in his work. Thoughtfully designed in every aspect, this home features an open floor plan and a seamless transition from indoor to outdoor living; nearly every room has a view of the courtyard and pool. My design direction was to create transitional spaces with modern brushstrokes.

The thoughtful design of this home includes double shutter-like doors flanking the main entrance leading directly into the outdoor entertaining space, which allows guests to enter without going inside.

Transitional décor can still be injected with warmth and subtle texture in furniture, art, fabrics, and finishes while maintaining a chic, streamlined aesthetic.

Transitional décor is a delicate balance between clean contemporary and comfortable traditional. The desired look is a chic, streamlined aesthetic with injections of warmth and subtle texture in furniture, art, fabrics, and finishes. In this home, weathered wood beams used in family spaces and the main bedroom instantly soften these large rooms, and we carried this theme through the furnishings. Other tactile finishes, such as velvet-upholstered sofas, linen-slipcovered chairs, natural-fiber rugs, and stone end tables increasingly add warmth and softness. Sheer white drapery provides texture on the walls as a backdrop for a moody landscape painting, and a gilded mirror overlays the panels. Apart from the emerald-green custom banquette positioned directly beneath suspended artwork, the home communicates primarily in shades of white; all the walls and much of the furniture are color free, but well-placed injections of black and gray punctuate the spaces. The ease with which spills or dirt mishaps can be noticed on light furniture made it imperative that all our upholstered pieces be covered in treated fabrics.

PREVIOUS OVERLEAF: Visual separation in an open plan is key. The round dining table with an alternating mix of chairs and the large, beaded chandelier divide the two living areas while giving the dining space individuality. OPPOSITE: A velvet-upholstered sofa, a wood-and-glass cocktail table, large brass floor lamps, and a natural-fiber rug work together to impart luxurious minimalism.

When working with a monochromatic palette and striving for restraint, the scale and proportion of each piece is especially critical.

When working with a monochromatic palette and striving for restraint, the scale and proportion of each piece is especially critical. Small, neutral seating options would look lost, so we chose generous upholstered pieces that demand attention. Large-scale floor lamps and a sizable square cocktail table add significant weight and presence. A gracefully stretched four-poster bed rising to meet a multi-armed iron chandelier effortlessly shrinks the height of the room without sacrificing aesthetic appeal. Everything works in synchronicity to achieve an uncluttered and appealing atmosphere with warmth and sophisticated ease, without any hint of sterile bareness. The home is fully appropriate for the bustle of family life and lively gatherings inside and out.

I always look forward to revisiting past projects; this one will likely receive a disproportionate share of visits. I am grateful for the upbringing I received in my hometown and the relationships I still maintain there. It's truly my first recollection of the joy of home.

Never underestimate the importance of scale in a large room. A sizeable square cocktail table surrounded by generously proportioned sofas and armchairs anchors one of the two living spaces. Using the same muted color palette and natural-fiber rugs in both areas links them together.

Architectural details of iron and wood throughout add diversity and interest to this tonal kitchen. A metal curio cabinet serves as decorative storage, and rope-hung pendants anchor the space.

ABOVE AND OPPOSITE: A polished leather armchair seated at the high-gloss-white breakfast table contrasts with the treated emerald-green velvet on the banquette, creating a multipurpose vignette for family dining or conversations.

OPPOSITE: The main bedroom continues the tonal theme with a mix of metal and wood. Here a vintage trunk is retrofitted with a lift for the TV when desired.
ABOVE: The pewter soaking tub serves as the artwork in the daylight-filled bathroom.

The moose-head mount, for the avid hunter in the family, serves as a focal point for the outdoor living as well as disguising the TV. The monochromatic scheme is a seamless continuation of the home's interior.

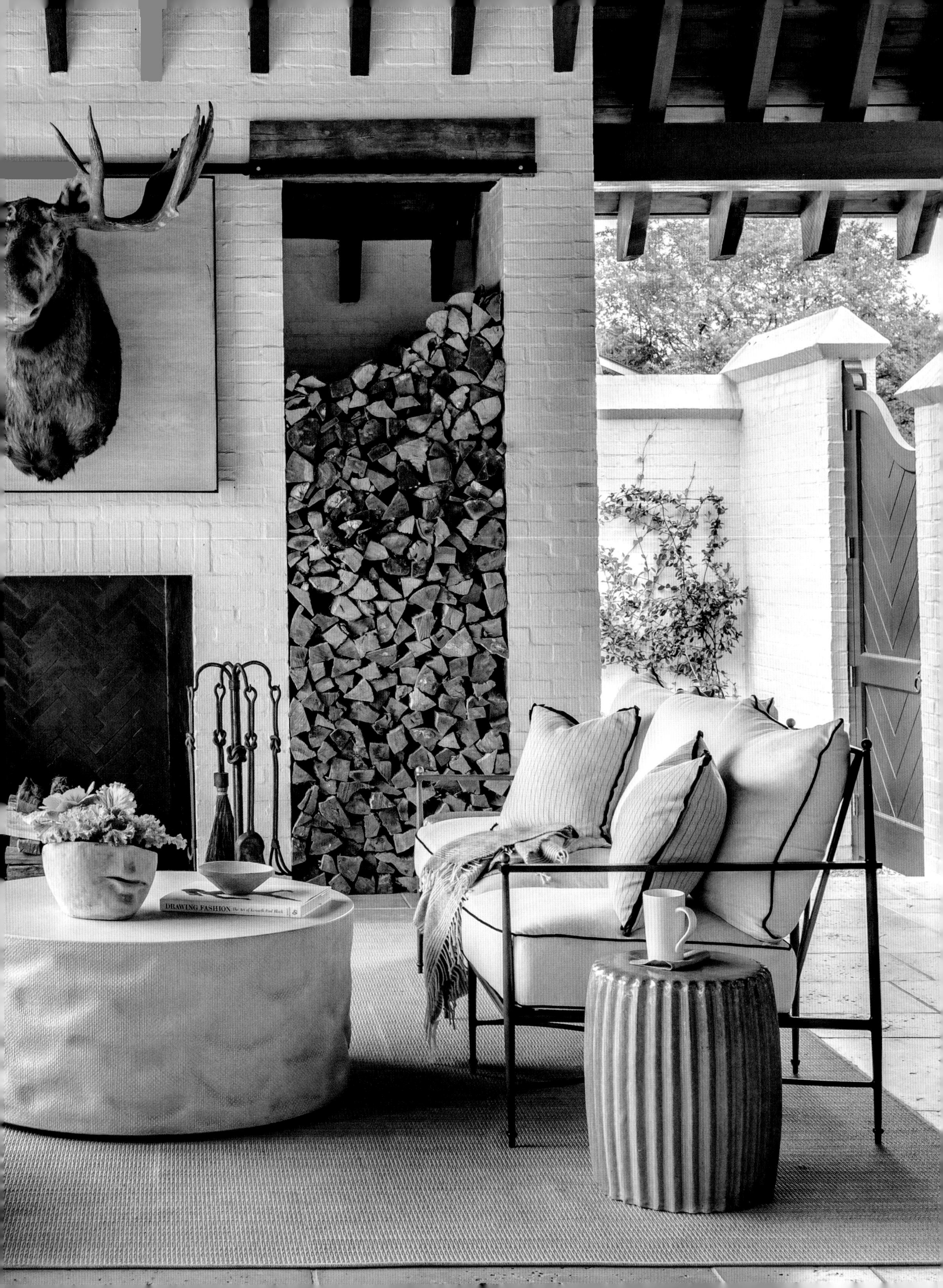
DRAWING FASHION The Art of Kenneth Paul Block

An Elevated Design

My greatest struggle is finding a balance between my work and spending time with my family. I absolutely love what I do every day, but nothing compares to the joy of intentionally looking my people in the face. Life is but a flicker in time and babies don't keep. I don't want to miss out on the impressionable moments while my children are still young. I think this is the reason so much of my work is driven by family life and the memories made during our time together—not because I have some magic philosophy or specific parameters, but because I truly feel the importance of our time together. I am honored to be a small part of helping create spaces for others' family time.

We often join projects in the preconstruction and planning phase and get to work with architects and builders to create an unfolding dream home from the ground up. Sometimes we are brought into an existing home, where we work within a given set of parameters to add personal and sentimental charm. Both are rewarding when the job is done, but the approaches are different from a design perspective.

OPPOSITE: A series of black-and-white photographs intentionally hung to overpower the antique cabinet add interest just inside the front door. The tone of this textural grass cloth wall covering sets the study apart as a masculine retreat. OVERLEAF: The family room shows off a pattern play of stripes, botanicals, and abstracts in blues, whites, and greens, creating a cheerful gathering place and easily connecting the palette of the outdoor spaces to the inside.

Sometimes, we work within a given set of parameters to add personal and sentimental charm to an existing home. Complete wardrobe changes aren't necessary when a new shade of lipstick provides just the right amount of pop.

The home on this exceptional, wooded, lakeside property featured a spectacular backyard for entertaining and offers a welcoming pool area for those steamy Southern summers. Our goal here was to elevate the spaces with a few tweaks and design tricks while adding thoughtfully chosen furnishings. Every space in this home was designed to support specific, whole-family activities.

A particularly special room already featured a performance stage (previously constructed by the client, complete with a theater curtain) where the children embarked on impromptu theatrical interpretations and whimsical dance parties. We played with the elevation to allow for better views of both the stage and projection screen. Clipped ceilings were softened by adding yellow striped draperies, and a trimmed valance along the sides of the sloping space created boundaries and divisions.

In a separate recreational room, we removed a closet to increase overall function and elevated one side of the floor to create theater-like seating. A large sectional sofa and a pair of chaise lounges accommodate adult gatherings for

The study serves as a destination place for working at home. Brass accents at the chandelier and picture lights, a vintage bottle collection displayed on the shelves, and an old leather desk chair harmoniously work together to add character and personality.

Humble textural pieces can be used as creative alternatives to expensive artwork and help to provide balance in more casual settings.

sporting events but are particularly comfortable for family movie nights. Custom cabinetry with a hidden refrigerator, icemaker, and storage are practical additions, but they also significantly enhance the aesthetics of the space.

Smaller, expressive tweaks took place in many of the rooms. Complete wardrobe changes aren't necessary when a new shade of lipstick provides just the right amount of pop. A grass cloth wall covering, a new paint color for the built-in bookcases, and brass picture lights provide a slight sophistication in the home office. Blue-slipcovered counter stools and burnished metal pendants gracefully update the kitchen. And a collection of weathered breadboards serves as sensible artwork for the walls in the cozy breakfast area. Humble textural pieces can be used as creative alternatives to expensive artwork and help to provide balance in more casual settings.

I often tell my children I am still learning to be a mom because I haven't previously been one. Getting to see how other families live and learning aspects of motherhood from so many of my clients is a blessing. When they describe how they want their houses to function in different stages of life, it gives me insight and provokes my thoughts for my own family.

The kitchen is open to both the family room and keeping room. Dark metal pendants anchor the island, while comfortable counter stools are made for conversations, quick meals, and occasional homework.

A large African textile adds color and texture to the daylight-filled keeping room.

A two-tiered iron-and-brass chandelier draws the eye up, and the finish complements the kitchen pendant lights. A collection of vintage breadboards adds texture and antiquity. A round pedestal table encourages family time, while a pretty tablecloth brings color and cheer to the morning rush.

ABOVE: In the main bedroom, a traditional ladder-back armchair adorned with dress-maker details is a soft and feminine complement to this space. OPPOSITE: A petite, round, antique table with curving lines and an aged marble top adds an airy touch in the sitting area.

ABOVE: In a daughter's bedroom, we dressed the twin beds with patterned valances and drapery to add dimension. A desk serves as a nightstand and provides a spot for homework. OPPOSITE: A hint of lilac in the bed draping complements the decorative patterns and creates a tonal focal point at each bed. OVERLEAF: A multipurpose space includes a unique stage area with a microphone and props at the ready. A generously proportioned, slipcovered sofa and an ottoman in a washable fabric allow for a crowd and easy upkeep. The striped, yellow drapery, complete with a hand-painted valance, on either side of the room helps give each space definition.

This playroom doubles for sleepovers as well as a stage for all imaginations.
The wall covering and geometric patterns are playful to serve the younger children
but classic enough to be timeless.

In the revamped entertainment space, we found room for a Ping-Pong/pool table. We added a counter in the redesign as a spot for snacks and drinks. The seating area beyond serves as the center for all sports and movie watching.

PREVIOUS OVERLEAF: When outfitting a large outdoor entertaining space, we take cues from the setting and the interiors and include a variety of organic styles and finishes. ABOVE AND OPPOSITE: All the décor speaks to the understated beauty of the outdoors. We used teak, stone, woven pieces, and a mixture of fabrics to complement the natural beauty.

Beach Happy

My husband and I have been vacationing in the same coastal area from the time our eldest daughter was a newborn, and I grew up going to the very same white-sand beaches. In fact, my most treasured childhood memories are from there, usually with cousins and other extended family in tow. I have loved keeping the tradition of joy at the beach and watching my babies develop their own love for the area.

As we considered purchasing this house, we saw loads of positives: a quiet neighborhood, a large and mostly undisturbed beach, and a coveted spot on a rare coastal dune lake with expansive views of the Gulf of Mexico. Conversely, the décor felt stuck in time and the house seemed void of any significant architectural features to accentuate this prime location. Aside from the house's physical location, there was little connecting the outside to the inside. In my opinion, this house was originally designed from the outside in, with little thought about the interiors, so we slipped in some simple architectural elements that made a huge impact.

Wood beams on the ceiling impart character and draw the eye up to appreciate the substantial height. A ventless firebox in the dining area adds an appealing focal point and enhances the home's year-round usability. Retractable window-wall systems provided seamless transitions to both the poolside

The location of our beach house provides the best of both worlds: it's on the lake with views of the ocean. We enjoy paddleboarding on still waters, and beachside fun is just steps away.

For this house, which felt like it had been originally designed from the outside in, we slipped in some simple architectural elements that made a huge impact.

courtyard on the ground floor and the breathtaking views of the upper porch on the Gulf side.

Finish changes also created an instant uplift. Stripping the cherry-stained wood foyer and wood ceilings throughout to reveal the natural tones lightened the overall color scheme. Changing to integrated kitchen appliances proved to be more functional and aesthetically crisp. Taller cabinetry offered more storage for reducing open clutter. The bold but airy antique upholstery table, masquerading as the kitchen island, gives even more storage but isn't overly intrusive or dense. The palette of blues, whites, and khaki allows nature to take the lead, while slipcovered sofas and warm wood finishes casually welcome visiting beachgoers.

Optimizing space in these "journey homes" allows for the inevitable invitation of children's friends, so we added bunk beds in the space reclaimed from oversized bedroom closets. Treated performance fabrics on all the upholstery and durable,

The home's color palette is introduced at the entrance by a patterned Oushak rug, an antique spindle bench covered in printed African mudcloths, and textural pillows. The antique mirror is one of the forever favorites in my collection. Washed-pine walls bring muted, beachy tones inside.

ABOVE: Striped linen wall covering contrasts against the black concrete sink in the small powder bath. OPPOSITE: A leather sofa, along with the washed wood ceiling, repeats the sandy tones, while the driftwood-like cocktail table lends a coastal vibe.

ABOVE: Large porches create a wonderful flow for indoor-outdoor living.
OPPOSITE: A washable slipcover on the sofa adds just the right casual, family-friendly note. An old trunk doubles as a cocktail table and provides practical storage.

ABOVE AND OPPOSITE: The antique dining table, with a beautiful, durable patina, expands to create more seating. Vintage, leather-upholstered chairs are easy to maintain for beach life and wet swimsuits. Here, one of two large iron chandeliers helps to break up the open floor plan and provides delineation in the space.

The revamped kitchen includes a new hood trimmed in brass, making a great focal point. Painting all the cabinetry a soft blue creates an understated beachy look. The marble backsplash and the vintage upholsterer's table serving as an island add both function and decoration.

222

Wood tones continue in the main bedroom on the ceiling, while woven nightstands and a patterned sisal rug accentuate the organic tone. The four-poster bed with custom bedding lightens up the dark wood finish. A faded blue stripe for the bed skirt and drapery is repeated on the vanity chair for a crisp, unified look.

ABOVE AND OPPOSITE: This bathroom was redesigned to maximize daylight. The glass-and-iron shower enclosure and sheer café curtains allow light to fill the space, while suspended mirrors reflect it. A reed-front wooden vanity with hidden drawers contributes to the airy feel.

OPPOSITE AND ABOVE: In our daughter's room, we mixed tonal prints with striped wall covering in shades of blue for a not-too-sophisticated, beachy flair. Painting the trim to bring out the wall covering tones adds a pop of color without being overpowering.

When you have a beach house, guests are a given. Treated performance fabrics on all the upholstery and durable, natural-fiber rugs make visitors all the more welcome.

natural-fiber rugs make visitors all the more welcome. Finally, I wanted the children to have special bedrooms; while youthful and beach happy in spirit, these spaces are not too childish, so older guests feel comfortable as well.

Writing this book has illuminated a level of self-reflection I hadn't previously taken the time—or had the time—to understand. During the process, and through examining my own emotions and feelings, I have been able to further appreciate not only the impact our team has made on our clients, but also the impact our clients have made on our team. More personally, I've realized that the serenity found near the water or in the mountains helps me enjoy my journey. I think we all have places where we feel more connected, more at ease. It could be a journey home where we get to spend a few special moments at different times, or it could be more consistently felt in the home where most days are spent. I hope our work inspires you to look more closely—and in more places—for the joy of home.

A bunk room serves as a wonderful children's space and a destination for little guests. Navy blue on the bunks sets this space apart, and striped drapery calms the room. The brass railing and ladder add a nautical hint. Framing children's artwork adds a personal touch.

Countless family meals are enjoyed on this porch. Teak works well in a coastal setting because it weathers beautifully. Dining chairs softened with slipcovers in a striped outdoor fabric join with a colorful tablecloth to bring a cheerful note to al fresco dining.

OPPOSITE AND ABOVE: The downstairs screened porch has a mix of seating options to ensure everyone has a place to perch. A blue-and-white palette always feels right, especially with a coastal backdrop. It's a favorite pairing that's timeless and easy to work with.

Acknowledgments

Putting together a book showcasing what I love doing every day involves the collaboration of many talented people, and I could not have done this without your dedication and friendship.

My heartfelt thanks to the staff of Ashley Gilbreath Interior Design. You work tirelessly to help make my visions and ideas a reality, and you helped keep our business moving forward while we also worked on this book.

Special gratitude to Meagan Rhodes, President of AGID. You are my heart and soul and absolutely one of my best friends who knows me inside and out. You are a cheerful and brilliant mind reader who is always fifteen steps ahead of me and keeping me on task. You have an amazing work ethic, and I would be completely lost without you.

Additional thanks to the following:

The incomparable book whiz Jill Cohen and her team. You listened to me and believed in this book from the start and were there to see it across the finish line.

The dynamic duo of photographer Emily Followill and stylist Eleanor Roper. You each have a brilliant eye and every image is beautiful. My trust in you was unwavering throughout the process, and you were an absolute joy to be around. Any day with you two never felt like work; it was always creative and simply fun.

My new friend and patient writing partner Alice Doyle for putting up with me and my erratic schedule with composure, understanding, and humor; my steady-eyed and kind editor Madge Baird and the rest of the Gibbs Smith team for helping me express my vision in words and images.

My book designer Doug Turshen and his associate David Huang, who took a set of images and made magic with them in every chapter. Your creative eye and depth of experience in creating an engaging visual presentation was so comforting throughout the whole process.

My longtime friend, the talented and supportive James Farmer for writing the foreword and for inspiring me with your graciousness, thankful spirit, and celebration of life. I'm so thrilled for your success, but most of all, I treasure your friendship, and I appreciate your thoughtfulness in everything you do.

My wonderful clients for giving me the ultimate privilege of entering your lives and the most sacred of places, your homes. Thank you for believing in me and my team to fulfill your dreams and help you create forever memories shaped by home. There is no greater honor.

The friends in this industry who I love like family and without whom I would be lost. You have gone above and beyond since day one. I am forever grateful for your love and commitment. You've taught me so much: Chris Edgar, Jim Gowan, Robert Hammock, Russ Hussey, Rusty Hussey, Mark Jordan, Dave Mills, Susie Mosley, John Phillips, Cole Reese, Mike Tatum, Sharon Wilson, and Steve Womble.

My parents, Emily and Ernie Freeman, I am so thankful for your love and support and the home you made for us. My siblings, Brian and Katie, I could not have dreamed for a better family. Our parents taught all three of us the importance of hospitality, thoughtfulness, attention to detail, and a strong work ethic. Mom and Dad, you made the joy of home a reality every day.

My precious children, Cates, Rett, and Liza, for helping me realize daily the irreplaceable importance of home. The welcoming arms and comfort of memories we make in love give me ultimate perspective and remind me how incredibly beautiful our heavenly home will be if we choose to measure the moments made with people we love and not the things that surround us.

Finally, my husband Barrett Gilbreath. You are my best friend, my greatest supporter, and my rock. You believed in me before I believed in myself and continue to do so every day with your patient and loving spirit. This book is dedicated to you. I couldn't have done this with you and I would not be me without you.

First Edition
27 26 25 24 23   5 4 3 2

Text © 2023 Ashley Gilbreath
Foreword © 2023 by James T. Farmer III
End papers: Uccello in aqua, courtesy Schumacher

Photographs © 2023 by Emily Followill, except as follows:
© 2023 by Laurey Glenn, pages 194–95, 198. 199, 200, 201
© 2023 by Jeff Herr, pages 9, 113, 128, 132–33, 134–35, 136, 137, 138–39, 171–85

Published by
Gibbs Smith
P.O. Box 667
Layton, Utah 84041
1.800.835.4993 orders
www.gibbs-smith.com

Designed by Doug Turshen with David Huang
Developed in collaboration with Jill Cohen Associates, LLC
Printed and bound in China

Gibbs Smith books are printed on either recycled, 100% post-consumer waste,
FSC-certified papers or on paper produced from sustainable PEFC-certified
forest/controlled wood source. Learn more at www.pefc.org.

Library of Congress Control Number: 2022941935
ISBN: 978-1-4236-6343-0